# BRYCE HARPER

BY ELLIOTT SMITH

SportsZone

An Imprint of Abdo Publishing
abdopublishing.com

abdopublishing.com

Published by Abdo Publishing, a division of ABDO, PO Box 398166, Minneapolis, Minnesota 55439. Copyright © 2018 by Abdo Consulting Group, Inc. International copyrights reserved in all countries. No part of this book may be reproduced in any form without written permission from the publisher. SportsZone™ is a trademark and logo of Abdo Publishing.

Printed in the United States of America, North Mankato, Minnesota
042017
092017

Cover Photo: Chris Bernacchi/AP Images
Interior Photos: Chris Bernacchi/AP Images, 1, 4–5; Josh Holmberg/Icon Sportswire, 7; Isaac Brekken/AP Images, 9; Alex Brandon/AP Images, 10–11, 19, 20–21, 25; Mike Janes/Four Seam Images/AP Images, 13, 14; Mark J. Terrill/AP Images, 16–17; Nick Wass/AP Images, 23, 29; Mark Goldman/Icon Sportswire/AP Images, 26–27

Editor: Todd Kortemeier
Series Designer: Craig Hinton

Publisher's Cataloging-in-Publication Data

Names: Smith, Elliott, author.
Title: Bryce Harper : baseball MVP / by Elliott Smith.
Other titles: Baseball MVP
Description: Minneapolis, MN : Abdo Publishing, 2018. | Series: Playmakers | Includes bibliographical references and index.
Identifiers: LCCN 2016962125 | ISBN 9781532111495 (lib. bdg.) | ISBN 9781680789348 (ebook)
Subjects: LCSH: Harper, Bryce, 1992- --Juvenile literature. | Baseball players --United States--Biography--Juvenile literature.
Classification: DDC 796.357 [B]--dc23
LC record available at http://lccn.loc.gov/2016962125

# TABLE OF CONTENTS

Bryce Harper

## CHAPTER 1

# A YOUNG STAR

The 2016 Major League Baseball (MLB) season had just begun. Bryce Harper stood in front of the home dugout at Nationals Park. His Washington Nationals were playing in their home opener. They faced the Miami Marlins. It wasn't just any home opener for Harper. He had been named the Most Valuable Player (MVP) of the National League for the 2015 season. A full stadium of Nationals fans was there to celebrate.

**Bryce Harper follows through on a swing during the Nationals' 2016 home opener.**

In 2009 Bryce was featured on the cover of *Sports Illustrated* magazine. That is pretty unusual for a high school athlete. It was the first time many fans heard about the future star. Bryce said he wanted to play in the majors by 18 or 19.

The MVP Award is given to the best player in each league. Writers who cover baseball vote on it. The award is one of the greatest honors a player can receive. Harper was just 23 years old. He was the youngest player ever to receive every first-place vote. He had a great season in 2015. Harper had a .330 batting average. He added 42 home runs.

Harper's teammates watched him play great all season. Now they watched and cheered from the dugout as he received the MVP. He proudly held the award over his head. Fans chanted, "MVP! MVP!" Harper couldn't help but smile.

It was a special day for Harper and the Nationals. And he sent the fans home with another memory. He hit a home run in the seventh inning.

Bryce Harper was born on October 16, 1992. He grew up in Las Vegas, Nevada. Baseball was a big part of his life from a young age. His older brother, Bryan, played the game too.

**Bryce rounds the bases during his sophomore year at Las Vegas High School.**

Their father worked in construction. Ron Harper laid steel in many of the city's hotels. But he also liked to coach baseball. He had a special drill to help his sons develop a great batting eye. He would "pitch" sunflower seeds for Bryce and Bryan to hit.

Bryce liked baseball. He wanted to play just like Bryan. So his parents signed him up for T-ball when he was three years old. He played against kids who were twice his age.

Bryce played other sports, too. But he knew he wanted to be an MLB player. *Baseball America* magazine called him "possibly the country's best 12-year-old hitter." At age 16, he was over 6 feet tall and weighed more than 200 pounds. Bryce had all the tools of a great player. He had a strong arm. He could run fast. And he had the power to hit home runs.

Bryce attended Las Vegas High School. He played catcher. He showed why he was one of the country's best young players. His statistics as a sophomore were amazing. His batting average was .626. In 115 games, Harper hit 14 home runs with 36 stolen bases. Word began to spread. He could be a very special baseball player.

Bryce was ready for a challenge. His parents came up with a plan to help his career. He graduated from high school two years early. He then went to the College of Southern Nevada.

At 16 Bryce took part in a home run derby. It was held at Tropicana Field. The Tampa Bay Rays play there. Using a metal bat, Harper hit the longest home run in stadium history. It traveled 502 feet and hit the back wall.

**Bryce prepares to bat while playing with the College of Southern Nevada Coyotes.**

That allowed him to play more games against better players. And his team played mostly with wood bats. They only used metal in the playoffs. It was another way Bryce could prepare himself for the big leagues. Pro players only use wood bats.

The plan worked. Bryce played one season of college baseball. He hit .443 and won the award for the best amateur player in the country. At age 17, Bryce was ready for the next step in his journey.

Bryce Harper

## CHAPTER 2

# PREPARING FOR THE MAJORS

Every year, teams gather for the MLB Draft. They choose from the best amateur baseball players in the country. The team with the worst MLB record gets to pick first. That was the Washington Nationals in 2009. They took pitcher Stephen Strasburg. They picked number one again in the 2010 draft. It was no surprise that they chose Bryce Harper. The Nationals now had two of the best young players in the game.

**Harper wears a Nationals jersey for the first time after being introduced as the team's first draft pick.**

The team decided to change Harper's position. He went from catcher to the outfield. Catcher is a tough position on a player's body. The Nationals thought moving Harper to the outfield would keep him healthier. He also could focus more on hitting. They felt it was the fastest way to get Harper to the majors.

Some baseball players wear black makeup called "eye black." Eye black helps them see better when it is sunny. Harper often wore big streaks of it on his face. He thought it looked cool and scared opponents. But Harper said he wouldn't wear as much in MLB.

Harper wasn't ready for the majors just yet. He started his career in the minor leagues. There, young players get to experience baseball as a job. It's not easy. They play games every day. They take long bus rides. The crowds can be small. And Harper struggled at first. He felt that he wasn't seeing the baseball well.

**Harper gets a lead off third while playing a minor league game with the Harrisburg Senators in 2011.**

A trip to the team eye doctor helped a lot. The doctor told Harper that his vision was poor. He suggested new contact lenses. It was just what Harper needed. He began to see the ball much better.

Harper finished the 2011 season at the Double A level. That is two steps away from the major leagues. He then played in the Arizona Fall League. Many young players use this league to get

**Harper watches the flight of the ball in a 2012 game with the Syracuse Chiefs.**

extra work in during the offseason. Harper was on a team with another future star. It was Mike Trout of the Los Angeles Angels. Their team won the league title.

The 2012 season was just ahead. Harper thought he had a good chance to make the Nationals roster. He was playing very well. But the team decided to be patient. He began the 2012 season at the Triple A level with the Syracuse Chiefs. He was just one step from the major leagues. His dream was close to coming true.

Harper thought he was ready. But he had to prove it while playing at Triple A. More fans began coming to his games. They hoped to see Harper play before he became a star in the majors. Playing in front of bigger crowds was exciting for him. He played 21 games for the Chiefs. Then Harper got the call he had been waiting for. He was moving up to the big leagues.

Harper is not the only ballplayer in his family. His brother, Bryan, is a left-handed pitcher in the Nationals' minor league system. The brothers played together for one season in college.

MONDO

## CHAPTER 3

# WELCOME TO THE SHOW

MLB is the best baseball league in the world. That's why it's called "the Show." On April 28, 2012, Harper made the Show. His first game was against the Los Angeles Dodgers at Dodger Stadium.

Reporters from around the country came to see Harper play. His family was also in the stands. Harper said he was not nervous before the game.

**Harper prepares for his first major league at-bat.**

He showed that he belonged. He got his first career hit in the seventh inning.

Harper was the youngest player in baseball at 19. He made sure to listen to veteran members of the Nationals. They had useful advice for him. He showed respect to opposing players. And he played as hard as he could.

Harper hit his first home run on May 14. Nearly every game, he did something to impress his teammates and fans. He was quickly becoming one of the most popular players in baseball.

Harper was named to the 2012 National League (NL) All-Star team. He replaced injured outfielder Giancarlo Stanton. Harper became the youngest position player to ever make the team. He didn't get a hit. But he called the game "an unbelievable experience."

Things were not always easy for Harper. He was still adjusting to MLB. In one game, he had no hits in seven at-bats. He struck out five times. But Harper never got down on himself. He knew there would be ups and downs as a young player.

**Harper comes home to score on a home run in the 2012 NL playoffs.**

The Nationals had not been a very good team. But things were starting to change. They were in first place. They had hopes of making the playoffs for the first time since 1981. Harper played a big role in turning the team around.

The Nationals finished with 98 wins. That was the most in the NL. Harper earned a surprise trip to the playoffs in his first season. Washington lost to the St. Louis Cardinals in the first round. But it was still a special year.

Harper was named NL Rookie of the Year. He finished the season with a .270 batting average. He hit 22 home runs. Those numbers were just a sign of things to come.

JACKIE ROBINSON AWARD
2012
ROOKIE OF THE YEAR
PRESENTED TO
BRYCE HARPER
WASHINGTON NATIONALS

## CHAPTER 4

# RISING TO THE TOP

Bryce Harper picked up where he left off to open the 2013 season. He hit two home runs on Opening Day against the Miami Marlins. He was the youngest player to accomplish that feat. Harper was only 20. But he was already one of baseball's best power hitters.

Harper suffered an injury during a May game in Los Angeles. He ran into the wall at Dodger Stadium and hurt his knee. He was placed on the disabled list.

**Harper shows off his NL Rookie of the Year award prior to the Nationals' first game of 2013.**

The injury made him miss 31 games. But Harper came back strong. He hit a home run in his first game back. He finished the first half of the season with 13 home runs.

Harper was chosen to compete in the 2013 Home Run Derby. His father pitched to him. He made it to the final round but lost by one home run.

Harper finished 2013 with a .274 batting average. He had 20 home runs. He had 58 runs batted in. But the Nationals missed the playoffs. Any chance of a fast start in 2014 ended quickly. In April, Harper suffered a serious thumb injury. It came following a triple he hit against the San Diego Padres. Harper slid headfirst and jammed the thumb into third base. He needed surgery. He had to go on the disabled list again and missed 59 games.

Harper finished the 2014 season with a .273 average. He hit 13 home runs. Washington won its division and made the playoffs. Harper played some of his best baseball there. He

Harper makes a sliding catch in a 2013 game.

hit three home runs and had four runs batted in. But it wasn't enough. The Nationals lost to the San Francisco Giants.

Harper's playoff performance set the stage for his amazing 2015 season. He hit three home runs in a game for the first time in May. He was among the league leaders in many categories. And he made the All-Star Game for the third time. He received

Harper had a short film made about him in 2015. Marvel Comics and ESPN teamed up on *1 of 1 Origins: Bryce Harper*. It is about the beginnings of Harper's baseball abilities. Home movies and comic book drawings help tell the story.

13 million votes from fans. That was more than any other NL player.

The 2015 season was the best of Harper's young career. Advanced statistics showed that he had the best season of any hitter in 10 years. But he was disappointed the Nationals did not make the playoffs.

After the season, Harper received an honor that meant a lot to him. He was voted Outstanding Player in the NL by his fellow players.

**Harper watches a home run sail over the fence during the 2015 season.**

34

## CHAPTER 5

# THE SKY IS THE LIMIT

Harper has achieved a lot at a young age. He made the majors at 19. And he continues to reach new highs. Harper hit his 100th career home run in April 2016. Later that year, the Chicago Cubs walked him six times in one game. That rare feat tied an MLB record.

Harper is one of the most popular players in the game. His Nationals jersey usually ranks in the top 10 in sales. He stars in a number of popular television

**Harper slides in safe at home in a 2016 game.**

commercials seen around the world. And his energy on the field makes fans stand up and cheer.

Harper also uses his fame to give back to those in need. He has hosted a Make-A-Wish patient at Nationals Park. He started his own charity called Harper's Heroes. The program helps children who are fighting cancer. Harper also created a series of limited-edition hats. Sales of the hats go to help cancer programs.

One of Harper's most interesting streaks ended after 415 games. In June 2015, the 22-year-old Harper finally faced a pitcher younger than him. The New York Yankees' Jacob Lindgren was also 22 but born five months later.

Harper has become one of baseball's great ambassadors. He represents the game off and on the field. He continues to work hard at getting better. But his top goal is to help his team win the World Series. The Nationals won their division again in 2016. But they suffered another first-round exit in the playoffs.

**Harper celebrates hitting a home run in 2016.**

Harper was the key piece in Washington's World Series hopes. Already an MVP, he had proven himself as one of baseball's biggest stars. Nationals fans hoped that his next achievement would be delivering them a championship. And with all of his talent, the sky truly was the limit for Bryce Harper.

## FUN FACTS AND QUOTES

- "It's what I've wanted since I was seven years old." —Bryce Harper, upon getting drafted by the Nationals in 2010
- Harper wears No. 34 in honor of Hall of Famer Mickey Mantle, who wore No. 7. Harper wore 7 as a youth. When 7 wasn't available, he switched to 16 or 34 because the digits added together equal 7.
- "You talk about faces of the franchise, you couldn't have a better ambassador not only for the game of baseball and Major League Baseball, but also this city and District of Columbia." —Nationals general manager Mike Rizzo on Harper
- Harper had his car customized to feature a bat rack in the trunk and the Nationals "Curly W" logo to replace the Mercedes symbol on the back.

## WEBSITES

To learn more about Playmakers, visit **abdobooklinks.com**. These links are routinely monitored and updated to provide the most current information available.

# GLOSSARY

**amateur**
Someone who is not paid to perform an activity.

**ambassador**
A representative or messenger.

**disabled list**
A list of players who are unable to play due to injury or illness.

**draft**
The process by which teams select players who are new to the league.

**feat**
A notable achievement.

**rookie**
A first-year player.

**roster**
The collection of players on a team.

**sophomore**
A second-year student.

**statistics**
A collection of numbers or data.

**tools**
In baseball terms, the skills players need to have. Throwing, hitting, fielding, and arm strength are considered tools.

**veteran**
A player who has played for many years.

# INDEX



## FURTHER RESOURCES

Goessling, Ben. *Washington Nationals*. Minneapolis, MN: Abdo Publishing, 2015.

Jacobs, Greg. *The Everything Kids Baseball Book*. Avon, MA: Adams Media, 2014.

Scheff, Matt. *Bryce Harper*. Minneapolis, MN: Abdo Publishing, 2016.